Children go to school to learn.

Different Types of Schools

Some schools are in cities.

Schools

Around the World

Clare Lewis

Chicago, Illinois

© 2015 Heinemann Library
an imprint of Capstone Global Library, LLC
Chicago, Illinois

To contact Capstone Global Library, please
call 800-747-4992, or visit our web site
www.capstonepub.com

Edited by Joanna Issa, Shelly Lyons, Diyan Leake, and
Helen Cox Cannons
Designed by Cynthia Akiyoshi
Original illustrations © Capstone Global Library Ltd 2014
Picture research by Elizabeth Alexander and
Tracy Cummins
Production by Victoria Fitzgerald
Originated by Capstone Global Library Ltd

Library of Congress Cataloging-in-Publication Data

Lewis, Clare.
  Schools around the world / Clare Lewis.
     pages cm.—(Around the world)
  Includes bibliographical references and index.
  ISBN 978-1-4846-0370-3 (hb)—ISBN 978-1-4846-0377-
2 (pb) 1. Schools—Juvenile literature. I. Title.

LB1513.L49 2015
371—dc23   2013040504

Image Credits

Alamy: Bill Bachman, 11, 23 (bottom), Jochen Tack, 10,
Robert Harding, 14, Steve Morgan, 8, 22 (bottom middle);
Getty Images: David Bathgate, 9, 22 (bottom right),
David Leahy, 5, Hugh Sitton, cover, NOAH SEELAM,
16, Ocean, 12, track5, 18, View Pictures, 6, 22 (top left),
XiXinXing, 19; Shutterstock: Brenda Carson, 1, Dmitry
Berkut, 20, 22 (bottom left), Hurst Photo, 15, back cover,
Ixepop, 24 (right), Jason CPhoto, 3, Juice Verve, 21,
Kozini, 2, Mega Pixel, 24 (left), Stocklite, 17; SuperStock:
Biosphoto, 13, 22 (top right), Exotica im/Exotica, 4,Stock
Connection, 7, 23 (top)

Contents

Schools Everywhere

Children go to school all over
the world.

Some schools are in the country.

Some schools are outside.

This school is on a boat.

Some schools are at home.

Some children talk to their teachers on the Internet.

How Do Children Get to School?

Some children go to school on
a bicycle.

Some children walk to school.

Some children go to school on a boat.

Some children go to school on
a bus.

What Do Children Learn at School?

Children learn to read and write.
Children learn to do math.

Children learn about other countries.
Children learn about art and music.

What Else Do Children Do at School?

Children meet their friends at school.

Children eat at school.

Schools are different all over the world.

What do you like to do at school?

Map of Schools Around the World

Picture Glossary

country place that is away from towns and cities

Internet way of using computers that allows people who are far away to share information

Index

Notes for parents and teachers

Before reading

Ask children why they think they go to school. Ask them if they have ever been to any other schools before. What things were similar? What things were different? Show children a globe or map of the world and identify the continents. Explain that children go to school all over the world, and ask them to think about how schools in the book are similar and different as they read the book.

After reading

- Review pages 12–15 about how children get to school. Ask children how they got to school today and make a class graph to record and compare the different ways.

- Point out the map on page 22 and identify the continents with children. Demonstrate how to use the map to identify the continent on which different photos from the book were taken. Ask children where the photo on page 9 was taken (Asia). Have children look at the photo and discuss or list what things are similar and different between that school and their school.

Note on picture on page 12: NEVER ride a bicycle without a helmet.